# yet, praise

A Collection of Poems on Suffering & Hope

Ashley K. Jones

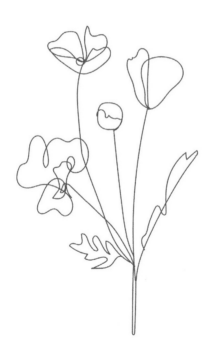

Yet, Praise copyright © 2021 by Ashley K. Jones. All rights reserved. Cover photography by Kelsey Verrill. Cover page art by Moriah Bender. Printed in the United States of America. No part of this book may be used or reproduced in any manner whatsoever without written permission except in the case of reprints in the context of reviews.

# Author's Note

In September of 2020, I looked in the mirror and noticed a lump under my collarbone. My dad & I rushed to Urgent Care where I underwent scans and biopsies. A few weeks later, I was diagnosed with Rhabdomyosarcoma—a rare, aggressive pediatric cancer.

In the months to follow, green chemotherapy chairs became my new office. Hospital waiting rooms became a second home. I met some of the most resilient children and parents who inspired me to keep fighting. Most of all, I witnessed the power of community to pour hope into the valley of suffering.

When hospitals paused the kids' holiday programs, I ached deeper— yet I could hardly get out of bed. It was my friends, family, and church community who sprung into action. Together, we supplied brand new tablets and Christmas gifts for the center.

In January, as a nurse took down my height and weight, I noticed a little girl  leaving the clinic hugging a new doll. The Childcare Coordinator approached me and smiled. "That was a gift *you* brought," she whispered. I shook my head because it was not just me. It was the labor of those around me who brought that gift into fruition.

It was *your love* that brought it together—and held me together—when I was crumbling under the weight of disease. This is only one of the many ways *you* have reflected the love of God to me and the next generation. And for that, I thank you dearly.

*One hundred percent of the proceeds from this chapbook will go into continuing efforts for children battling cancer.*

## Acknowledgments

I put together this collection of poems rather quickly as I awaited a difficult tumor removal surgery with great risks. Once again, dear friends made it possible.

I want to thank Kelsey Verrill for giving me a beautiful photograph for the book cover and Moriah Bender for her lovely drawing on the cover page. I also want to thank Lizzy Sullivan for her mentorship in formatting & design. And thank you to Abby Dengler who stayed up with me the night before the operation editing away.

I hope this encourages you, wherever you find yourself in your story, to acknowledge the gravity of pain, recognize the weight of suffering, and also find a reason to sing.

This collection is dedicated to my loving sisters, Ava Jones & Shamar Hudson, my amazing dad, Andre Jones, my dearly missed mom, Arlene Jones and my sweet aunties, Mary Veal, Brenda Lotridge, & Kathleen Stavrinides.
And to my dear friends; Abigail Dengler, Meghan Parsons, Carlyn Hawkinson, Katie Dy, Christine Gonzales, Alex Russ, June Marie, Michael Brown, Andrew Gibson, Campbell Ong, Angela Pham, John Michael McCaffery, Rebecca Pope, Jessica Vitagliano, Nicholas O'Connor, Stacie Perez, Ella Moore, Brianna Young, Ashley Thompson, Abigail Gaines, Maris Gentry, & Kelsey Sherman.

## table of contents

*night's ache*................................................................1

*a new day*...................................................................2

*mirrors*.......................................................................3

*yellow*........................................................................4

*curled on the couch*......................................................5

*neighborhood walk*.......................................................6

*at the sink*...................................................................7

*savor*..........................................................................8

*nourning in the afternoon*...............................................9

*yet, praise*..................................................................10

*daytime television*........................................................11

*afternoon scroll*...........................................................12

*late lunch*...................................................................13

*breaking news*................................................14

*quarantine*................................................15

*love note for the afternoon lull at 3pm*................................16

*Papa's shelf*................................................17

*love note for the evening blue's*................................18

*mercy*................................................19

*courage*................................................20

*bruises*................................................21

*unraveling*................................................23

*advocacy*................................................24

*clarity*................................................25

*evergreen*................................................26

*even when*................................................27

*hope at dusk*................................................28

*tomorrow*................................................29

A.K.J.

## night's ache

two pillows cover the floor
where my feet should be.
I tossed and turned last night
unable to fall asleep.
Instead, I scrolled atop my bed
whilst a blue light shrouded me.
I looked forward to morning glow.
I pined for birdsong.
for the sunrise is
a holy embrace
when the ache of the night is long.

yet, praise

**a new day**

sunrise came like a breath.
I'm underwater
& yet I've surfaced.
when I kick my legs, I unravel.
take my hand oh God as I paddle ahead
into the unknown again.

A.K.J.

## mirrors

mirrors show new weight.
the state of my thighs.

curves rising high.
catching my sighs.

but the mirror cannot show me
the beauty I've gained inside.

as I've grown,
I've shown the mirror...

I am more than my size.

yet, praise

## yellow

when I'm struggling to understand,
the peace that transcends
comes through.

like a ray of light on a dark feeling,
turning yellow what was blue.

A.K.J.

**curled on the couch**

sunlight pours through our window in one thick ray.
draping onto the couch where I lay.
though I want to stay...

I'm beckoned upwards again to continue today.

my feet hit the ground.
& it is the sound of the *thud*
which awakens me to this:

I am alive & I will only have this moment once.

yet, praise

## neighborhood walk

dawn waning
bluer skies arrive with birdsong
nipping cold
my skin raises
bee's humming
phone buzzing
vibrations
alarms unheard
I looked up
two doves
spread their wings
strolling through
leaping onwards
each step an act of worship

A.K.J.

**at the sink**

dishes calling.
*water falling over plates.*
It's routine & lousy.
until the simplicity is serendipity
when everything else falls away
& suddenly, the sink is a quiet place to think.
I drink old memories.
I let them linger.
Today, I am an opera singer.
I dream in bubbles of soapy rainbows.
I wash away soggy carrots, play in translucent suds,
& sing in a cloud of steam.
I am a woman with cancer.
but at the sink, I am a woman with a dream.

*yet, praise*

**savor**

I pour green tea in my mug.
with my hands, I hug the cup.
*savor the first sip...*
I was told.
there is only one.

A.K.J.

## **mourning in the afternoon**

the pain comes like a wave,
unexpected and violent.
where is the light at the end of the tunnel?
crawling forward on my knees towards the toilet,
I press on.
I vomit.
where is the light at the end of the tunnel?
I carry memories on my back,
photographs stacked like plaque.
there is light at the end of the tunnel &
in the middle.
I know you're here too.
I feel your warmth.

*yet, praise*

a bold, enduring motto.
a quiet desert grotto.

a song which plays...
even so, we are okay.

A.K.J.

## daytime television

daytime television asks one thing of me.
it pleads for my *time.*
and grief, in its delusions,
makes me believe I have too much of it.
grief likes to disguise itself as nothingness.
but it is not nothing.
if it were, I would not
need entertainment's Novocain
to appease it.
and yet, when I turn off the set,
I come into silence & it's holy.
the time I spend
missing my mom's warm bear hugs,
I don't regret.
though I cannot fast forward the pain of it.
I can feel the significance.

yet, praise

## afternoon scroll

I once scrolled to compare.
but today, I scroll to share.
I scroll to celebrate, to accept
the invitation to care
about the person on the other
side of the screen.
maybe they are suffering, like me.

A.K.J.

## late lunch

filling my body with nutrients is right.

we were not meant to be starved nor stuffed.

I won't suppress pain with food or the lack of it.

instead, I'll write.

I'll do what it is that I love.

*yet, praise*

**breaking news**

the Capitol laid in disarray.
Congress walked back on that day.
and counting never looked so brave.

counting never looked so brave.

A.K.J.

## quarantine

though my schedule is on hold,
I keep growing old.
time still passes by
though the gatherings
we've used to mark it slowed.
It still goes.
and we still grow.

we still grow.

*yet, praise*

## love note for the afternoon lull

perhaps, there are more people
rooting for you than you might believe.

just maybe there's someone you can picture
who will relieve the stress you're feeling.

perhaps, there is one person you can recall
who reminds you:

though this world can be scary,
you are brave.

you are strong.

A.K.J.

## Papa's Shelf

when I do not know how to see myself,
He pulls kind words off the shelf.
When Abba speaks,
I can see again.

He never runs out of love.

*yet, praise*

## love note for the evening blues

beloved, you are not alone.
God is not distant.

in his love,
you have a home.

## mercy

when I fail, your mercy rushes in.
your kindness falls upon me like rain on my skin.
and I remember:
*your love has no end.*
no depth or height could pull us apart.
you've been close from the start.
Your faithfulness
strips the weapon formed against me.
so, we can just be.
standing in the tender rain.
what was dirty is clean again.
your mercy has no end.
no end.

yet, praise

## courage

emergency exits like ships at sea
on my radar internally.
buzzing through the *what if* flurry
buying a bag of chips,
I'm searching for the red words.
sitting alone, I'm desperate for the assurance
if I screamed, I'd be heard.
as if, every time, their fleet could carry me.

no, I'm tucked under the shadow of his wings.
sung over by the King of Kings.
when I cannot see in front of me,
there is ground.
and there is He.
He who hears me.

A.K.J.

## bruises

when the bruises on my skin
come from my own hand,
You do not condemn.
somehow, You give me the grace to rest
as you rescue me
from myself.
You remind me again.

*I am beloved.*

yet, praise

*You are beloved.*

A.K.J.

**unraveling**

competition is unraveling at the need before us.

there is a collective hum of collaboration.

a pursuit of justice.

a longing for more mercy.

a craving for understanding.

what once was a cacophony has become
a symphony.

we are together.

I will never forget the sound of this.

*yet, praise*

## advocacy

to take a knee in solidarity is to say with your movement, you're a part of the Movement.

the one much longer than headlines & captions.

you call others to take action, to fight for their neighbor and to labor for the sake of change.

and you say to the wounded, I am no longer apathetic.

I am an advocate for your belovedness.

A.K.J.

## clarity

on this road, this I know:
there is much I don't.
I beg for clarity to come
so I can move knowing what's ahead.
but there's a fog instead,
unknowns so thick they taste like dread.

yet, I am sure of this:
the steadfast love of the Lord never ceases.
and by the power of the Holy Spirit, he's close.
He's near and comforting my weary bones on this road.
this I know.

this I know.

yet, praise

**evergreen**

You lift my head tenderly.
from my window, I can see.
the trees are evergreen.

A.K.J.

**even when**

even when I am afraid, your love comes.
even when I have little faith,
as small as seed barely seen,
your love still meets me.

It reaches down to rescue me from

    the
       shifting
           sea.

my weary body finds refuge in your wings and sings,
*holy are You, King of Kings.*
*You are trustworthy.*
*You are worthy.*
*Your mercies do not cease.*

*yet, praise*

## hope at dusk

hope is a four letter word.
an explicit grouping of letters heard.
a sound which won't give in to despair.
it sees the possibility for love &
goes there.

A.K.J.

## tomorrow

I don't know what tomorrow will bring.
but I know the song you sing...

Peace.

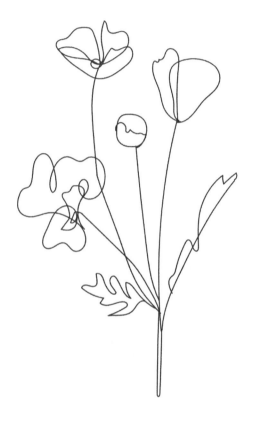

To connect with Ashley, drop her a note
on Instagram @ashleykendalljones
or visit her website at
ashleykjones.com.

Made in the USA
Las Vegas, NV
04 March 2021